MUMMERS, MAYPOLES AND MILKMAIDS

To Our Chum Ant
in anticipation of
his visit to All Cannings
in the very near future.

Christmas 2014

Judith
and
Richard

SARA HANNANT

MUMMERS, MAYPOLES AND MILKMAIDS

A JOURNEY THROUGH THE ENGLISH RITUAL YEAR

MERRELL

LONDON · NEW YORK

Contents

Full Circle: English Seasonal Rites and Rituals

A chance encounter with Deptford Jack-in-the-Green in south London in 2006 prompted my fascination with seasonal rites in England. Intrigued and inspired by what I had stumbled on, I began to photograph the unfolding events. A man dressed entirely in green was decorating a 3-metre (10-ft) cylindrical frame with foliage. Then, several people placed a crown of flowers on top and raised the structure high enough for a tall man to crawl inside. Concealed by the greenery, he moved in a circular motion, and a crowd gathered and shouted, 'Jack's alive!', on which cue musicians in Edwardian costume began to play a joyous traditional song called 'Rogues' March'. Locals followed as the procession moved through the residential streets. When it reached the River Thames, a man wearing a toga and a laurel headdress made a speech honouring the river as the city's lifeblood. To herald the coming of summer he asked two women dressed as a Lord and Lady to throw garlands of flowers into the river. Horns sounded and cheers rang out, and folk dancing and music followed, including a maypole dance performed by young children holding coloured ribbons. The procession then continued through the neighbourhood (opposite), stopping at various pubs, where the music and dancing carried on (see pp. 30–37).

This May Day ritual is thought to have evolved from a custom initiated by milkmaids (see p. 36). By the 1750s chimney sweeps had joined in the women's parade, making rough music with their brushes and shovels. Over the years the processional costumes worn by the sweeps evolved from garlanded headdresses into a large leaf-covered armature encasing the entire man, later known as 'Jack-in-the-Green'. In the 1980s members of Blackheath Morris Men discovered a photograph taken in 1906 by press photographer Thankful Sturdee (1852–1934), captioned 'An old May Day custom – Jack-in-the-Green'. It featured the Deptford Morris team, Fowlers Troop, which was named after one of the sweeps in the photograph. Inspired, the Blackheath Morris Men revived the troop and Deptford Jack-in-the-Green. In 2006, to mark the centenary of the photograph, the organization Rediscovered Urban Rituals invited locals to join Fowlers Troop and participate in a parade dressed as the characters pictured.

Reminiscent of the ancient celebrations of Saturnalia or the medieval festivals of Misrule, the revived Jack-in-the-Green represented a reinvented 'Merrie England' played out in contemporary London. I was now compelled to discover what other events there were to mark seasonal change. Looking at the year as a turning wheel of seasons helped me to seek out likely locations

for the dramatization of natural processes: wassailing ceremonies to toast the orchards in cider-making regions; summer solstice celebrations at sacred sites; and such agricultural customs as the Straw Bear, once common on Plough Monday (see p. 21) in Whittlesey, Cambridgeshire. I have always been very interested in folklore, customs and nature-based spirituality, but I had not realized that such practices are so widespread, nor that they play such an integral role in the cultural identity of present-day England.

For this book I have travelled to rural and industrial locations throughout England to photograph regional rituals. It is not a comprehensive survey of communal customs, but reflects my personal journey through the passage of the year. I have photographed costumed processions, symbolic and sacred drama, traditional dance, street music and fire ceremonies that celebrate the cycles of nature. Many of these customs incorporate ancient imagery, and are kept alive by local communities. I have included traditions that follow the cycles of the pastoral year, and rites and rituals that celebrate a pagan

heritage. Sometimes, people with differing interests converge at the same event, such as Lammas in Eastbourne (pp. 92–95), which attracts people for reasons ranging from the social to the spiritual. My aim has been to capture the essence of people and place, moments of abandonment or collective expression, and the humorous juxtapositions found in English culture. To explore notions of national identity I decided to photograph only in England. Since 2006 I have photographed more than fifty rites and rituals, from the Abbots Bromley Horn Dance (pp. 108–11), which is claimed to date from 1226, to such relatively new inventions as the environmental charity Common Ground's annual Apple Day (pp. 124–25).

English popular culture has been chronicled by many photographers, notably Sir Benjamin Stone (1838–1914), who in 1899 staged photographs of the Abbots Bromley Horn Dance for the first volume of his *Pictures* series, *Festivals, Ceremonies and Customs: Relics of Merrie England* (1906). The book fostered nostalgia as a form of resistance to urbanization and industrialization. It was the discovery of Stone's book in a junk shop in 1966 that prompted the photographer Tony Ray-Jones (1941–1972) to embark on his long-term project *The English: A Day Off*, documenting English culture before the advent of Americanization. Although inspired by both men, I have differentiated my work by photographing the coexistence of tradition and modernity, and showing how folkloric practice has evolved in response to changing social needs.

The people I have photographed believe that rituals can forge a dynamic connection between past, present and future. Just as seasonal rites follow the rhythm of the year and are not seen as separate from everyday life, so communities often regard their participation as 'just what we do'. The growing number of revivals and reinventions of previously banned local traditions confirms the enduring desire for a communal belonging to time and place. Attendance and involvement vary greatly; bonfire night in Lewes attracts 20,000 visitors, for example, while the Yorkshire midsummer Burning Bartle is an intimate gathering of around fifty local people.

On my journey I encountered and photographed many interesting and helpful people, without whom the project would have been impossible. I feel privileged to have witnessed so much unofficial culture and to have been welcomed into so many communities. I recall being roused from sleep on May Eve by the hypnotic rhythm of the May Song played beneath my window in Padstow; the sharp whack of a pig's bladder on the back of my leg from the Fool at the Abbots Bromley Horn Dance; and the sight of my face marked in red by Red Leicester Morris Men. I have eaten delicious fertility cake in Bampton and apples fertilized by erotic dancing at Beltane in London. I have been chased by Penglaz (opposite) along the harbour wall in Penzance, and am delighted to have accompanied the Bacup 'Nutters' (below) 'to the bitter end' on their day-long boundary-to-boundary dance in the snow. I am proud to have symbolically cast off the past year and honoured the dead at Samhain in Glastonbury, to have run into the flames at Ottery St Mary and to possess a piece of the Carshalton Straw Jack for luck.

Tar Barrel Parade
Allendale, Northumberland
1 January

Just before midnight on 31 December, men in fancy dress hoist large whisky barrels of ignited tar on to their heads and parade around the village. On returning to the marketplace they cast the barrels into a huge bonfire, creating a cascade of flames. At midnight the crowds sing 'Auld Lang Syne', then there is dancing and the tradition of the first-foot, where householders invite costumed 'guisers' (men in disguise) to be first over the threshold in the New Year. Such a visit is thought to bring good luck for the next twelve months. Some locals believe that the fire tradition developed out of a Methodist night-time service in 1858, when torches were used to illuminate the band's music, while others consider that ritually burning out the old year to welcome in the new relates to earlier midwinter festivals once commonplace throughout the United Kingdom.

Mummers' Day
Padstow, Cornwall
1 January

The term 'mummers' in its broadest sense means 'people in disguise'. It is thought that mummers were first recorded in the thirteenth century as 'Momoeri', referring to a traditional form of Greek theatre in which performers wear festive masks or disguises. In the past, when working people put on popular entertainments – such as folk plays, music and dance – for money, food or drink, they wore masks or blackened their faces to avoid being recognized by potential employers. Mummers' Day occurs in Padstow twice a year: on New Year's Day and on Boxing Day. Local musicians blacken their faces, wear clothes similar to those of African American minstrels and perform minstrel and plantation songs as they go through the streets, stopping at local pubs along the way. Such bands as these were common following the minstrel craze that swept the country after 1836. The Padstow tradition, previously called 'Darkie Day', has recently been renamed 'Mummers' Day', and participants believe that it celebrates the liberation of slaves from ships docked in the town. Some of the performers claim solidarity with the slaves in their celebration, while others express a wish to continue the traditional guise of a black-faced character prevalent in midwinter festivals.

Wassailing the Orchard
Worthing, West Sussex
5 January

'Wassail', Old English for 'your health', was said when passing the ceremonial drinking bowl or cup; the reply was 'Drinkhail'. From this tradition developed the wassailing of the orchard, to wish the trees health and abundant crops in the forthcoming year. Cider is poured on the roots, and cider-soaked toast is tied to the branches to 'feed' the tree; a gun is fired to awaken the orchard and ward off evil spirits (left). Musicians play while everyone sings the Wassailing Song. The crowd then makes as much noise as possible to frighten any bad spirits; this is sometimes called 'apple howling'. Afterwards, much cider is drunk, both in celebration of the previous year's harvest and in anticipation of the next. Wassailing ceremonies vary from village to village. Often, a man and a woman dressed as a King and Queen lead the song or the processional music, and the Queen is lifted up to hang the cider-drenched toast as a gift to the tree spirits. The crowd recites:

Here's to thee, old apple tree,
That blooms well, bears well.
Hats full, caps full,
Three bushel bags full,
An' all under one tree.
Hurrah! Hurrah!

In Worthing this custom is performed by members of Sompting Village Morris (above) with local people.

Twelfth Night Celebrations
Bankside, London
6 January

Members of the Original Shakespeare Company formed the Lions Part to enliven traditional English seasonal rituals for contemporary audiences. On Twelfth Night – the end of the Christmas festivities and the customary day for wassailing – a celebration is held on the South Bank in London. The Holly Man, described by the theatre company as the winter manifestation of the Green Man from pagan myths and folklore, appears from the River Thames. Covered in foliage, he is said to embody the fecundity of nature, and wassails (toasts) the people and the river in an old tradition encouraging a fertile year ahead. The Globe Theatre is wassailed in like fashion. Afterwards there is a performance by the Bankside Mummers, culminating in the crowning of two people selected from the crowd to be King Bean and Queen Pea. This once-popular London custom echoes the Christian festival of Epiphany, which occurs on this day and commemorates the manifestation of Christ to the Magi.

Straw Bear Festival
Whittlesey, Cambridgeshire
13 January

The late medieval custom of the Straw Bear, revived in Whittlesey in 1980, was once common in English towns. On the Tuesday after Plough Monday (the first Monday after Epiphany, and the traditional start of the agricultural year), farmers would transform one of the local men into the Straw Bear by covering him in their best straw. Led by an attendant keeper, the Whittlesey bear parades and dances around the town accompanied by more than 250 dancers, musicians and other performers. The following day the bear effigy is burned at the 'Bear Burning' ritual. Originally, agricultural labourers asked for 'beef, tobacco and beer' in exchange for this entertainment, and as a result the festival was banned in 1910 for being a form of begging. A Whittlesey resident of German origin has forged a connection with a similar straw bear in Walldürn, Baden-Württemberg, where it parades on the day before Shrove Tuesday. Since 1999 the Walldürn and Whittlesey bears have attended reciprocal events.

The Pig Dyke Molly troupe (left), named after a local ditch, was formed in the 1990s and performs at the Whittlesey Straw Bear Festival. It is renowned for its black-and-white costumes, distinctive music and a style of Molly dancing that is robust, lively and loud. The dancers explain that the term 'Molly', common among the dance teams found in the Cambridgeshire Fens, describes a man dancing in women's clothing (from the so-called Molly Houses recorded in seventeenth- and eighteenth-century London, where transvestites could meet and drink). Annual rites for the return to work focused on Plough Monday, and, in East Anglia, ploughboys would decorate a plough and push it round the village, calling at houses to perform Molly dances in exchange for money. The lads sometimes ploughed up the gardens if they were not welcomed. Dancers might wear such disguises as face paint,

goggles or animal heads so as not to be recognized by their employers.

During the winter Leicestershire Morrismen change their kit to tattered jackets and bowler hats decorated with pheasant feathers, paint their faces red and become known as Red Leicester Morrismen (see pp. 6–7) to perform Border Morris dances at the Whittlesey Straw Bear Festival. These dances originated in the border areas of Herefordshire and Wales, and are wilder than the Cotswold dances performed by the side (or team) in the summer. The Morrismen's red-painted faces refer to the application of red raddle (an ochre dye) to rams' bellies by sheep farmers, so that the ewes are marked during the mating season.

Above: The Baden-Württemberg Straw Bear visits the travel agent, Whittlesey, Cambridgeshire.

Imbolc Fire Festival
Marsden, West Yorkshire
7 February

Since 1993 the people of Marsden have heralded the coming of spring with a community fire festival originated by Duggs Carre and Angie Boycott-Garnett, folklore enthusiasts who work for the local council. The festival has grown into a pyrotechnic display with fire sculptures, a torch-lit procession, music and dance. The word 'Imbolc' derives from the Old Irish *I molg*, meaning 'in the belly', and refers to the pregnancy of ewes. It is commonly believed that Imbolc was originally a festival of weather divination for the lambing season, dedicated to Brigid, the pagan goddess of poetry, healing and smithcraft. Brigid later became known as St Brigid, and Imbolc became the Christian St Brigid's Day. As both goddess and saint she was associated with holy wells, sacred flames and healing, and so fire and purification were traditionally an important aspect of the festival. By lighting candles the people hoped magically to ensure the sun's warmth over the coming months.

The Britannia Coconut Dancers of Bacup

Bacup, Lancashire
22 March

Local stories claim that the dances and costumes of the Britannia Coconut Dancers originate from Moorish pirates, who are thought to have settled in Cornwall some two hundred years ago before moving to Lancashire to work in the mines. On Easter Saturday, accompanied by the Stacksteads Silver Band, the dancers are led through the town from boundary to boundary by Dick Shufflebottom the whipper-in, so called because he carries a whip or whistle. Seven varieties of dance are performed: five garland 'spring ritual' dances in square sets, in which each man carries a curved garland decorated with red, white and blue flowers; and two 'nut dances', the Thowd Cash and the Figures. Each dancer wears maple-wood discs, or 'coconuts', on his hands, knees and belt, and during the dance he strikes them together in time with the music. They resemble the protection worn by miners on their knees and elbows when crawling along narrow seams. The dancers say that their blackened faces may reflect a pagan or medieval belief that disguise avoided identification by evil spirits, or may simply derive from the mining experience itself.

Biddenden Dole

The people of Biddenden annually bestow gifts in the name of the conjoined twins Elisa and Mary Chulkhurst, the 'Twin Maids', who were supposedly born in 1100. At the age of thirty-four one of the sisters died from an incurable disease, and the remaining twin died six hours later. The proceeds from their estate enabled the distribution of bread and cheese to the poor, and funds are still provided to locals in need. Biddenden cakes, bearing the impression of the Twin Maids and their names, age and year of birth, are also given away to all on Easter Saturday. The cakes, which are made from flour and water, are meant not to be eaten but to be kept as souvenirs.

Jack-in-the-Green
Deptford, London
1 May

Blackheath Morris Men and friends revived Deptford Jack-in-the-Green in the early 1980s, drawing inspiration from a photograph of 1906 by Thankful Sturdee (see p. 8). Historical information in the book *The Jack-in-the-Green* (1979) by folklorist Roy Judge has also shaped the current celebration. Illustrations and diary entries from the sixteenth and seventeenth centuries describe how people made garlands of flowers and leaves to wear as headdresses in May Day processions. Various works guilds would compete to make elaborate costumes, and in the late eighteenth century the chimney sweep's garland became so big it covered the entire man, who later became known as Jack-in-the-Green. It is customary for attendants called 'Bogies' to guide the Jack through the streets, often dancing and singing as they process. Jack is thought to be the embodiment of man and nature celebrating the return of summer.

Offering flowers to the Thames.

The Deptford Jack-in-the-Green procession crosses the Millennium Bridge, accompanied by musicians of Fowlers Troop (left), and passes Monument Underground station in the City of London.

Jack-in-the-Green, Deptford

To coincide with the year's first large yield of milk, milkmaids would dress neatly and balance a borrowed silver plate on their head, piled high with a pyramid of silverware, ribbons and flowers (opposite). Accompanied by bagpipers or fiddlers, they would dance from door to door to collect tips from their regular customers. Carrying milk churns and flowers, the women would cry 'Milk below!' up at the houses, and children would follow behind, dancing. 'Bunters', or women who worked as rag-pickers, would join in the parade, making a parody of the milkmaids by carrying milk pails and garlands made of brass, and dancing lewdly in the hope that they would also be given money.

May Day
Padstow, Cornwall
1 May

Musicians play the May Song as hobby horses (or 'obby 'osses) bow, twirl and sweep through the village goaded by a 'teaser' (a man or woman with a decorated club). Occasionally the music changes almost to a dirge, and the horses sink slowly to the ground, to be roused again by the teaser's dancing caress, the beating of drums and the crowd calling "Oss! 'Oss!' It is believed that dancing and singing with the 'Osses will bring good luck and fertility. Hobby horses, or model horses, operated by a person concealed within or half exposed as a rider, were common in early medieval May Games. The people of Padstow suggest a variety of possible origins for their ritual, from the Celtic festival of Beltane (see pp. 62–65) to a clifftop display used to frighten enemies. Local history has it that in the nineteenth century licentious cavorting around the Old 'Oss prompted the Temperance Movement to construct the Blue Ribbon 'Oss. Both 'Osses conceal a man under a frame draped with black oilskins. His head, which protrudes from the centre of a large black disc with a symbolic horse's head and tail on either side, is covered with a mask representing the rider. It is believed that if a woman is caught underneath the 'Oss, she will become pregnant within a year. On May Day all those born in Padstow proudly wear white with red or blue accessories to indicate their allegiance to either the Old 'Oss or the Blue Ribbon 'Oss. At midnight the Old 'Oss returns to its stable in the Golden Lion Inn, and the crowd sings the Farewell Song with much emotion.

May Day

The Padstow Mayers' Song sums up the
day's festivities, which begin the night
before with singing in the streets. At
midnight all eighteen verses of the
Night Song (below) are sung to rouse
particular residents from their beds.
Throughout May Day itself the Day Song
is sung alternately with the Night Song.
Both have the same opening verse:

Unite and unite and let us all unite,
For summer is a-come unto day,
And whither we are going we will
    all unite,
In the merry morning of May.

Rise up, Mr —, I know you well a-fine,
For summer is a-come unto day,
You have a shilling in your purse and
    I wish it was mine
In the merry morning of May.

All out of your beds,
For summer is a-come unto day,
Your chamber shall be strewed with
    the white rose and the red,
In the merry morning of May …

Sweeps Festival
Rochester, Kent
4 May

Rochester Sweeps Festival is a modern revival of an old tradition. May Day was traditionally a workers' holiday, enabling many chimney sweeps – including children – to participate in a parade of elaborate costumes (one of which was the 3-metre/10-ft leaf-clad armature later to be known as the Jack-in-the-Green; see pp. 30–37). After the passing in 1875 of the Climbing Boys Act, which made it illegal for young boys to clean inside chimneys, boys no longer took part in the festival, and its popularity waned. Celebrations in Rochester stopped in the early 1900s. The local historian Gordon Newton revived the tradition in 1981, organizing a small parade accompanied by a 2-metre (7-ft) Jack-in-the-Green. The festival is now supported by Medway Council and attracts many working chimney sweeps, more than sixty Morris sides and entertainers from throughout the United Kingdom.

Jack-in-the-Green

Hastings, East Sussex
5 May

In 1983 Mad Jack's Morris (opposite) revived the custom of Jack-in-the-Green in Hastings. The event is now the biggest of the several existing Jack-in-the-Green festivals, and attracts thousands of participants and spectators. A parade featuring giants, Morris dancers, fire-eaters, Bogies (overleaf, and see p. 31) and musicians leads Jack to the top of the castle hill, where he is ceremonially slain. His crown is sliced off and his foliage is thrown to the crowds; everyone scrambles to catch a piece to keep for good luck.

Maypoles were the focal point of many May festivities. To celebrate the coming of the fine weather for planting, a young tree would be cut down and placed with great ceremony at the centre of the village, stripped of its branches and decorated with garlands of flowers and flags, perhaps to honour the life-giving properties of tree spirits. The maypole dance may derive from ancient fertility rites, but it is not actually documented until after the later Middle Ages; the ever-popular notion of the maypole as a phallic symbol is in fact post-Freudian. In 1644 the Puritans banned maypole ceremonies as 'heathenish vanity' based on 'superstition and wickedness', and it is widely accepted that the current form of maypole dancing, using ribbons suspended from the top of a pole, first appeared as a spectacle in the stage production of *Richard Plantagenet* by John Thomas Haines in 1836. This captured the enthusiasm of Conservative politicians who wished to rekindle the harmonious spirit of 'Merrie England' that is supposed to have prevailed in medieval times. Such official authentication of this reinvented tradition resulted in its acceptance as an old English custom, and maypole dancing, which is mostly performed by children, has subsequently become widespread on the stage and at fetes and festivals.

The Hal-an-Tow and Flora Day

Helston, Cornwall
8 May

The Hal-an-Tow is a ritual drama performed in the street by a raucous cast of more than 250 people of Helston. The play incorporates elements of local and global history, including references to the Spanish Armada and such characters as St Michael (the patron saint of Cornwall), St George and the dragon, Robin Hood, Friar Tuck and Aunt Mary Moses (possibly the Virgin Mary). The first performance of the day begins at 7 am. The Hal-an-Tow Song clearly indicates the nature of the play:

Hal-an-Tow, jolly rumble, O!
For we were up as soon as any day, O!
And for to fetch the Summer home,
The Summer and the May, O!
For Summer is a-come, O!
And Winter is a-gone, O!

Locally the Hal-an-Tow is associated with Flora Day. Flora was the Roman goddess of flowers, and was connected to the spring. Being a fertility deity, she is linked with the renewal of the cycle of life.

The Hal-an-Tow and Flora Day

The people of Helston mark the arrival of spring by decorating the streets with greenery and taking part in processional dancing accompanied by the Helston Town Band. Smartly dressed couples dance at 7 am and 5 pm, while the dances for the younger people begin at 9 am, with both girls and boys wearing white.

The Furry or Floral Dance, pictured top left, is led by the mayor and starts at noon, threading between local shops and houses, allegedly bringing good luck. The men wear top hats and tailcoats, and the women evening dress. All are adorned with sprigs of lily of the valley, Helston's symbolic flower. Flora Day is in the spirit

of old summer feasts, and serves to unite the community. It was established by 1600, and its name is thought to derive from the Cornish *feur*, or 'holy day', similar to the Latin *feria*. Local records show that the Victorians banned the original Flora Day festival for its drunken revelry, and invented the current, more controlled celebration. The Floral Dance, for which it is now famous, was introduced in the 1920s and remains a fine example of Cornish processional dancing; it occurs at the same time as the Hal-an-Tow.

The New Lammas Lands Defence
Committee, based in Leyton, north-east
London, invites members of the local
community to walk the boundaries of their
common land and celebrate the annual
ritual of Beating the Bounds. Local history
reveals that during Rogationtide (the three
days before Ascension Day, which is forty
days after Easter Sunday) parishioners and
clergy would walk the parish carrying ritual
willow wands, which they would beat
on the ground at the edge of the parish.
Currently, each year a different faith leader
blesses the willows, which are decorated

with ribbons. Following tradition, ten *thegns*
(Old English for attendants) are elected
to watch for misdemeanours. At significant
parish boundaries children are turned
upside down and their heads gently
touched on the ground to 'imprint the
location on their minds'. The walk begins
with a ritual to pacify the waters at the
oxbow of the Old River Lea, then the group
proceeds to beat the bounds northwards
beside Walthamstow and Leyton marshes
and onwards to Dagenham Brook, where
the willow wands are cast into the water
and the ribbons kept for luck.

The Children's 'Oss.

Hunting the Earl of Rone
Combe Martin, Devon
25 May

Tom and Barbara Brown, who revived the Hunting of the Earl of Rone in 1974, claim that the festival had been banned since 1837 for licentiousness and drunken behaviour. On the spring bank holiday the costumed Grenadiers, Hobby Horses (pp. 60–61), Fool and villagers hunt for the Earl of Rone. Once found, the earl, played by a small child wearing a sacking costume and primitive mask, is paraded through the village (p. 59, top) and frequently 'shot' by the Grenadiers, only to be revived by the Hobby Horses and the Fool. At the final shooting, on the beach, he is not revived, and his costume is ceremonially cast into the ocean (p. 59, bottom). Local legend claims that the character of the earl represents Hugh O'Neill, Earl of Tyrone, who was forced to flee Ireland in 1607 and was shipwrecked in the nearby bay, Rapparee Cove. Hiding in the woods and surviving only on ship's biscuits, he was eventually captured by a party of Grenadiers sent from Barnstaple. Some people regard the custom as a remnant of medieval May Games; others like to think of it as the evolution of a pre-Christian scapegoat ritual.

Beltane
London
28 May

The Celtic festival of Beltane occurs at the beginning of the pastoral summer, when livestock herds were traditionally driven to their summer pasture, and marks the beginning of the bright half of the year. Beltane is considered by Pagans to be a Sabbat, one of the eight solar holidays. The London revival of this May festival has been in existence for more than ten years and attracts hundreds of people from throughout the United Kingdom. Festivities begin with a Pagan Pride Parade through Bloomsbury (left), with costumed characters and giants in medieval garb representing gods and goddesses (above). The crowd then gathers in Red Lion Square to celebrate the changing season with song, dance, drama and ritual. A dance in the form of a spiral winding through the fountain (overleaf) has become an integral part of the festivities.

Garland Day

Castleton, Derbyshire
29 May

Annual celebrations to mark the restoration of the monarchy in 1660 by King Charles II occur on Oak Apple Day (see pp. 68–69) in Castleton. Early morning preparations include a small group of men knotting wild flowers on to a large beehive-shaped frame called the Garland. Women make a special posy, known as the 'queen', to be placed on the top. The Garland weighs approximately 30 kilograms (66 lb) and is worn on the upper body of a man dressed as the king in Stuart uniform, riding on horseback through the village accompanied by his female consort riding side-saddle. (Until 1957 the consort was a man in woman's clothing.) Morris dancers lead the procession to the marketplace, where schoolgirls dance around the maypole. At each pub they pass the girls dance the Garland Dance (a form of Morris dance) while the Castleton Silver Band plays the Garland Tune. Meanwhile, the king approaches the church gate, where the 'queen' – deemed to be too pagan – is removed, and then rides on to the church. The Garland is hauled up the church tower, where it remains on display. Since 1916 the king has ridden onwards to place the 'queen' on the war memorial, at which point the band plays 'Abide with Me'. The crowd then dances its way home through the streets.

Oak Apple Day
Great Wishford, Wiltshire
29 May

Horns are blasted at dawn as locals gather oak boughs from Grovely Forest (right, top). Later, four women go to Salisbury Cathedral, accompanied by villagers, and present armfuls of oak to the dean, shouting 'Grovely!' several times. A service in the cathedral culminates in the granting of commoners' rights, which allow locals to collect firewood from the forest. Outside the cathedral the women perform a traditional folk dance, the Great Wishford Faggot Dance (opposite), carrying faggots, bundles of oak branches tied with bands of bark. Returning to Great Wishford, the dancers lead a procession carrying a banner bearing the words 'Grovely! Grovely! Grovely! And all Grovely! Unity is Strength!' Men carry the finest oak boughs, as rated by local judges, and are followed by May queens (right, bottom), musicians and local people in fancy dress. On 29 May, a national holiday from 1660 to 1859, the restoration of the monarchy by King Charles II is commemorated. The customary wearing of sprigs of oak leaves is symbolic of his escape from the Roundheads (Oliver Cromwell's Parliamentarian army) by hiding in an oak tree during the Battle of Worcester on 3 September 1651.

Whitsuntide
Bampton, Oxfordshire
31 May

It is claimed that Morris dancers have performed in Bampton every Whitsuntide for 500 years. There are currently three Morris sides in Bampton: the Bampton Traditional Morris Men, the Traditional Bampton Morris Dancers and the Bampton Morrismen. All dance in the streets, squares and private gardens from 9 am until dusk to the accompaniment of fiddles, melodeons, accordions, pipes and tabors. Each team includes a Fool carrying a bladder on a stick, thought to be an ancient fertility talisman, and a Sword Bearer (above), who carries a fruitcake impaled on a rod symbolizing a sword and distributes pieces to the crowds for luck. Folklorists influenced by the anthropologist Sir James Frazer (1854–1941), in particular his book *The Golden Bough* (1890), regarded Morris dancing as a form of ancient fertility ritual. Scholars suggested that the name came from 'moorish', and the blackened faces common to the festivities resembled the Arabs of Spain, thereby placing the origins of Morris in southern Europe. Recent research suggests that it can be traced back to the masques and entertainments of the royal courts of Europe about 1500. It is thought that the dances later spread to the streets, and became associated with seasonal festivities (see also p. 104).

Regional variations include Cotswold, Border and Molly dancing, North West Morris, Rapper Sword and Longsword. Dances may feature sticks, swords, bells, handkerchiefs and clay pipes, among other things. Many Morris sides also perform mummers' plays at Christmas and New Year. Costumes are traditionally inspired, and often incorporate a locally significant badge or symbol.

The Shoe Tree
Buxton, Derbyshire
2 June

Tree dressing, or decoration, has long
been practised throughout the world
for a multitude of reasons, including the
once prevalent belief that trees possess
life-giving properties. Wreaths, ribbons,
rags and other objects are suspended
in commemoration, to win favour for
the sick or to bring good luck. Buxton
teenagers created the Shoe Tree in the
summer of 2006 by throwing pairs of
shoes, tied together by their laces, into
the highest branches of the tree. Local
explanations of the shoe tree include
a communal ritual, rebellion, a practical
joke or to signal a drug dealer's territory.
Shoes may also symbolize the journey
through life, and those that form shoe
trees are often inscribed with greetings,
love poems and details of accomplishments
to represent a collection of personal and
shared experiences.

Well Dressing
Ashford in the Water, Derbyshire
3 June

Well dressing was once known as 'well flowering', and is believed by historians and local people to have pagan origins. Since much of the Peak District is porous limestone, water was frequently in short supply, and it is thought that offerings were made to water deities both in gratitude and in request. Banned by early Christians as water worship, the tradition was appropriated by the Church in the fourteenth century. From May to September the people of Ashford in the Water, one of the many Derbyshire villages that participate in well dressing, decorate wells and springs with pictures made out of local plant life. Carefully picked flowers and plants in intricate designs are embedded in clay-filled wooden trays mounted in wooden frames. The villagers work together for hours in secret on the designs, often through the night, before proudly revealing their creations. Local clergy bless the wells by shaking a sprig of rosemary dipped in holy water over them; prayers and hymns follow.

Filly Loo
Ashmore, Dorset
18 June

This revived midsummer celebration has been held since 1956 on the Friday closest to 21 June. It is thought by the organizers that the name 'Filly Loo' may be a corruption of the French *la fille de l'eau* (maiden of the water). The evening features dancing by White Horse Morris, live music by the Hambledon Hopstep Band and junior folk dances by Steps in Time accompanied by a Green Man. At dusk a torch-lit procession of six antlered horn dancers is accompanied by Maid Marian, a Bowman, a Hobby Horse and a Fool, who perform a variation of the Abbots Bromley Horn Dance (see pp. 108–11) to a solo melodeon in a minor key. The dance emulates the rutting of male deer during the mating season, and the performers believe it symbolizes the burgeoning fertility of summer. Finally, everyone gathers to encircle the village pond, holding hands for the last dance.

The Mayor of Ock Street
Abingdon, Oxfordshire
19 June

Each year, on the Saturday nearest to 19 June (originally the first day of the annual horse fair), the residents of Ock Street in Abingdon are invited by Abingdon Morris to elect the Mayor of Ock Street. The role of a Mock Mayor is very similar to that of a jester: to challenge the civic mayor and represent the townspeople's point of view. Once elected, the Mayor is ceremonially presented with his regalia and carried along Ock Street in a chair decorated with flowers. The procession continues through the town, stopping at pubs along the way to participate in Morris dancing and watch performances by local and visiting sides.

In 1700 some local men fought over the horns of a roasted ox in the arketplace. The Ock Street men won possession, and so the horns remain a symbol of Ock Street; they are also the insignia of the Abingdon Traditional Morris Dancers, who will not dance without them. The local people believe that touching the horns will bring good fortune. The regalia of the Mayor of Ock Street includes a rosewood cup, which is said to have been carved from a cudgel used in the fight.

Summer Solstice
Stonehenge, Wiltshire
21 June

Senior members of the Council of British Druid Orders celebrate the high point of the year's cycle on the longest day by conducting a Summer Solstice sunset ceremony. Attended by a gathering of hundreds of people, the Archdruid places an offering of flowers in the cauldron of fertility to symbolize the fruitful union of the Sun King, who is at the peak of his powers at midsummer, and Mother Earth, who is at her most fertile and abundant. Many Druids practise and cultivate the performance of seasonal rituals, meditation, solar and lunar knowledge, and the re-enactment of ancient truths through sacred drama. Arthur Uther Pendragon, Chief of the Loyal Arthurian Warband and Archdruid of the Isle of Britain, Rollo Maughling of the Glastonbury Order and members of the Secular Order of Druids were instrumental in the campaign to reopen Stonehenge to the public for the summer solstice. Controlled access was granted in 2000, and approximately 21,000 people now gather annually to watch the sun rise.

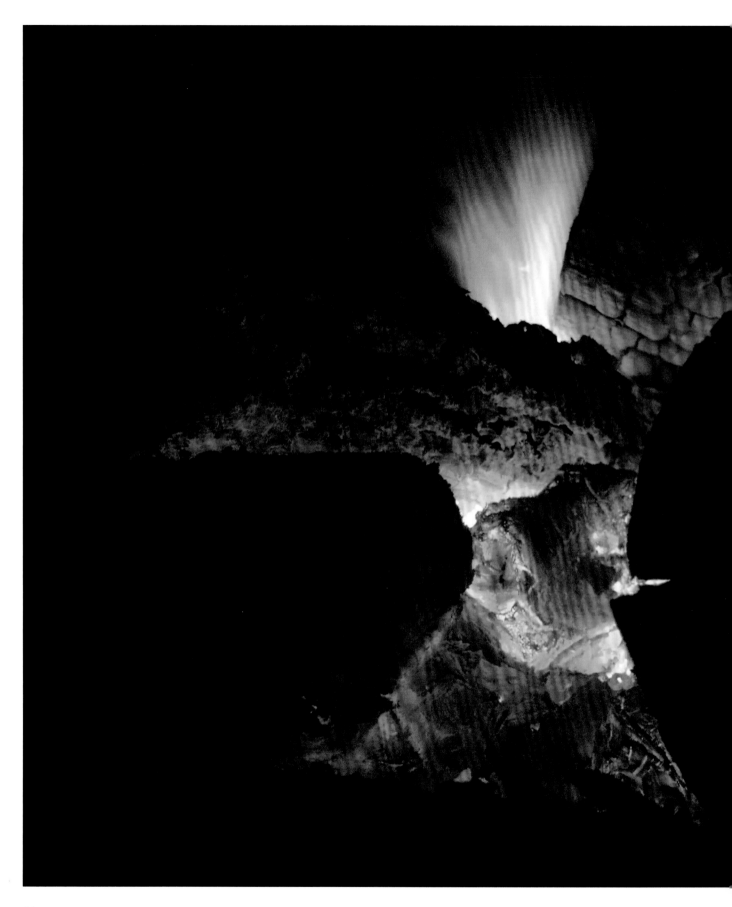

Midsummer Fire

Bow, London
24 June

As the historian Ronald Hutton explains in his book *The Stations of the Sun* (1996), ceremonies involving burning wheels, the most common symbol of the Sun, are recorded as taking place throughout Europe since ancient times. Pagan festival celebrations in Aquitaine in south-western France, for example, involved rolling a flaming wheel down a hillside to a river, then taking the charred embers to the temple of a sky god. Early medieval midsummer customs in England also revolved around fires, feasting and torch-lit pageants, occurring during the period between the Christian feasts of St John the Baptist and St Peter's Eve (24–28 June). At this time of year crops were most vulnerable to blight, animals were prone to diseases and humans were at risk from such insect-spread infections as bubonic plague, malaria and typhus. The flames, ashes and smoke were thought to bring blessings, purification and protection. Fires might be carried around the fields, cattle were driven through the embers and people leapt over the flames for luck. The lighting of fires to mirror the fierce heat of the Sun at its strongest and most long-lived is seen by some neo-Pagans as a celebration of the triumph of light and warmth over darkness, marking the high point of the Sun before the days begin to shorten and it becomes lower in the sky, bringing winter. The wheel is also considered to be symbolic of the Sun's passage through the turning seasons of the year.

Madron Well

Penzance, Cornwall
25 June

According to Cheryl Straffon, the author of
*Fentynyow Kernow: In Search of Cornwall's
Holy Wells* (1998), sacred wells were once
perceived as a direct route into Mother
Earth; the waters were understood to
be a source of life and fertility, a potent
manifestation of the spirit of the universe.
Celtic people used these wells for healing
and divination, particularly at midsummer.
The healing powers attributed to the
spirits that were thought to inhabit the
wells were later transferred to Christian
saints. Rituals were adapted and customs
arose to cure ailments and express wishes
for a happy life. The future was told by
throwing a pebble or a pin into the water,
with the number of bubbles said to reveal
the years before matrimony. Crosses were
also floated, and the response of the water
would – in the manner of the tossing
of a coin – be interpreted as the answer
to a specific question (if the cross sank, for
example, it might be taken to mean 'no').
Today, pilgrims make offerings of flowers,
stones or money, and tie rags to bushes
to encourage good health.

Golowan Festival

Penzance, Cornwall
26 June

Until as recently as the 1890s the people of Penzance celebrated midsummer by lighting fires on the hilltops and rolling flaming tar barrels through the streets. The authorities then outlawed the festival because of rising insurance premiums for the business community, but in 1992 local artists and schools revived a festival, Mazey Day, to coincide with Golowan, the midsummer feast of St John. This has grown into ten days of performances, including a midnight appearance of Penglaz, a tall 'Obby 'Oss bearing a horse's skull. The revived Penglaz was introduced to the festivities by Cornish piper Merv Davey, and is based on descriptions by Penzance antiquarians. The name 'Penglaz' refers to the mast- or pole-style 'Obby 'Oss peculiar to the Penwith region of Cornwall and first described as part of nineteenth-century midwinter festivities. The revived Penglaz is accompanied by a 'teaser', a woman who goads the 'Oss with a decorated club. She is known locally as the 'Bucca Gwidden' (spirit of light), and leads the 'Oss and the crowds in a serpentine dance along the quayside. The movements of the 'Oss can be wild and unpredictable, exciting the crowds.

Lammas

Eastbourne, East Sussex
4 August

The word 'Lammas' derives from 'loaf mass', the name of an old celebration traditionally held at sunset on 1 August with the cutting of the first corn. In Ireland, the ancient harvest festival was known as 'Lughnassah', after the Celtic sun god Lugh. The ritual was later appropriated by the Church, and has more recently been reclaimed by the modern Pagan movement. Eastbourne has held a day of Lammas celebrations in August since 2001, including a procession with giant puppets of Celtic gods, ritual, music, dance and stalls throughout the town. The ceremony starts with a dance performed by Hunters Moon Morris (right), symbolizing the death and rebirth of John Barleycorn, the personification of the summer's grain harvest from an old English folk song of that name. A rite follows to give thanks for the harvest and to ask for a plentiful year to come.

Puppet-maker and Eastbourne resident
Mel Myland made these two giants
specifically for the town's Lammas parade.
The male giant represents Herne, the
legendary antlered figure who is said to
haunt Windsor Forest. He is related in
folklore to the Celtic god Cernunnos.
The female giant represents Andred, a
Celtic lunar deity commemorated in the
Romano-British name for the fortified
settlement at nearby Pevensey: Anderida.
The giants are made from wicker and
papier-mâché on a backpack frame and
are operated by concealed 'carriers',
who make the giants appear to parade
and dance.

The Straw Jack
Carshalton, Surrey
13 August

Invented by local people in 2004 and organized by the drumming band RumpleDrumskin, this August ritual revives ancient customs that commemorate the last corn crop of the year. The Straw Jack is a 3-metre-high (10 feet) wooden structure covered in straw and decorated at the top with flowers. A man concealed inside is guided around by such costumed characters as the Squire, the Rat-Catcher, the Scarecrow and the Corn Dollies. Together with drummers and traditional musicians they process through the streets of Carshalton. The day culminates in a feast, more music and the ceremonial burning of the Straw Jack effigy. Before the fire is lit, people are invited to take a piece of the Jack for luck.

Burning Bartle

West Witton, North Yorkshire
24 August

A straw figure named Bartle, with hair
made of sheep's wool and light bulbs
for eyes, is carried from door to door.
A crowd gathers to replenish the carriers
with alcohol and hear the chant that tells
of Bartle's demise:

On Penhill Crags he tore his rags,
At Hunter's Thorn he blew his horn,
At Capplebank Stee he brak his knee,
At Grassgill Beck he brak his neck,
At Wadham's End he couldn't fend,
At Grassgill End he made his end.
Shout, lads, shout!

Bartle is then stabbed and set alight at
Grassgill End. One West Witton legend
tells of a swine- or sheep-stealer named
Bartle; other stories link Bartle to
St Bartholomew, on whose feast day the
custom occurs. During the Reformation,
locals allegedly attempted to hide their
statue of St Bartholomew from officials,
but the statue met the fate described
in the chant. Other stories connect Bartle
with ancient end-of-harvest customs
involving the burning of corn gods, or
with scapegoat rituals.

Rush-bearing Festival
Sowerby Bridge, West Yorkshire
2 September

Rush-bearing, the ceremonial taking of rushes to churches for floor covering, was common in Lancashire, Cheshire and West Yorkshire during the Middle Ages. The tradition fell into decline at the beginning of the nineteenth century, when stone floors were introduced. People in the town of Sowerby Bridge revived the tradition in 1906, and the current two-day festival was initiated in 1977. A team of sixty men dressed in panama hats, white shirts, black trousers and clogs (fitted with irons to accentuate their rhythmic steps) pull the rush cart around the town using ropes and wooden poles, while a young woman sits on the top and waves at the crowds who line the streets (pp. 102–103). A leader at the head of the team instructs the rush-bearers with a whip or whistle, and musicians and several teams of Morris dancers follow behind. In recent years a number of other Morris sides have also revived rush-bearing ceremonies, most notably the Saddleworth Morris Men. These days it is common for men to build and pull the rush carts. However, this has not always been the case: in King James I's edict *The Book of Sports* (1618), there is a reference to women pulling the carts.

Morris dancing has long been an important part of rush-bearing festivals. The Morris Ring, a national organization formed in 1934, asserts that Morris dancing is for men only; the Morris Foundation and Open Morris, formed in 1975 and 1979 respectively, welcome both women and men. Most of today's Morris clubs are 'revivals', started after such collectors as Cecil Sharp (1859–1924) recorded much of England's traditional music and dance in the early twentieth century. Mary Neal (1860–1944), who worked initially with Sharp, formed the Espérance Girls Club in London in 1896, where she taught dances to young working-class women. While Sharp aimed to preserve dances 'intact', Neal was instrumental in developing the modern form of Morris dancing. The all-female Hebden Bridge Hill Millies was formed in 2002 and performs traditional dances at festivals throughout the country, including its local rush-bearing festival.

Scarecrow Festival

Norland, West Yorkshire
3 September

Norland's scarecrow festival began
in 2000 and is run by the community.
Every year a different theme is chosen
and prizes are awarded for the best
scarecrows. Famous for being the
guardians of the harvest, scarecrows
are positioned outside houses, schools
and shops in Norland, as well as in the
fields. The Suffragette scarecrows shown
here were part of the festival in 2007.

Horn Dance

Abbots Bromley, Staffordshire
9 September

The Abbots Bromley Horn Dance is widely claimed to be one of Britain's oldest surviving traditions. The dancers assert that there are records of a performance at Barthelmy (or St Bartholomew's) Fair in Abbots Bromley in 1226. On the Monday after 4 September the performers attend an early-morning service at the church of St Nicholas, where they collect the reindeer antlers for their dance. Six Deer Men (pp. 110–11), a Fool, a Hobby Horse, a Bowman and Maid Marian then perform a rhythmic dance to music provided by a melodeon and a triangle. The Fool (left) leads the procession for 16 kilometres (10 miles) through Abbots Bromley, carrying a pig's bladder (a fertility talisman) and an alms collection box. A young man dressed as Maid Marian (opposite) carries wooden ladles, which are referred to as 'old women's tools' and said to symbolize fertility. The Horn Dance is performed at specific locations, including several farms, where hospitality is lavished on the dancers in the belief that doing so will ensure a plentiful harvest. All the money collected is given to charity. The troupe is welcomed by Lady Bagot to perform on the raised grounds of the Bagot ancestral home, Blithfield Hall, where they are watched by crowds of local people who gather below at the boundaries of the estate.

Crab Fair

Egremont, Cumbria
15 September

According to its organizers, the Egremont Crab Fair started in 1267 when Thomas de Multon, Lord of the Barony of Egremont, granted a charter for the fair and gave crab apples away to local people. This grew into an annual festival – held on the nearest Saturday to 18 September – featuring traditional sports, entertainment and the World Gurning Championship. The parade of the apple cart, where apples are thrown into the crowds on Main Street, continues to be popular with the community, but rather than celebrating local produce and employment the event now uses specially imported apples. These days few of the locals work on the land; in recent years most were employed at the nearby Sellafield nuclear plant.

Autumn Equinox

Avebury, Wiltshire
Primrose Hill, London
21 September

Merlin of England, of the Loyal Arthurian Warband, retires to the trees after participating in an autumn equinox rite at Avebury stone circle in Wiltshire. The autumn equinox, known as Mabon or Harvest Home, when day and night are of equal length, is the second festival (after Lammas; see pp. 92–95) of the harvest season; the third is Samhain (see pp. 128–29). There are many different orders of Druids, both national and local. Members of the Loyal Arthurian Warband celebrate the eightfold wheel of festivals that mark the annual cycle of the Earth's seasons. Four of these fall on the equinoxes and solstices, and are known as 'quarter days'. To mark these occasions some members perform public rituals at Avebury, Primrose Hill in London and Stonehenge (see pp. 82–85). At the autumn equinox, thanks are given for the fruits of the harvest. Traditionally farmers would harvest their crops by the nearest full moon to the autumn equinox, known as the Harvest Moon, and as part of the celebration livestock would be slaughtered and the meat preserved for the winter. The autumn equinox is regarded as a time to reflect on what has been achieved and learned during the past year, and to plan for the future.

Members of the Druid Order, also known as the British Circle of the Universal Bond or the Ancient Druid Order, conduct an annual ceremony on Primrose Hill in London to mark the autumn equinox. The members, who are called Companions or Companions of the Light, wear white robes and process to the top of the hill to form a circle. The ceremony features banners, a sword-bearer, the blowing of a horn, the reading of a scroll and representations of the four elements (earth, air, fire and water). A woman representing the Celtic goddess Cerridwen enters the circle accompanied by two female attendants carrying baskets, from which they scatter the flowers and fruits of the harvest. Traditional rituals are practised to honour the principles of nature and their application in everyday life. Despite the date of its founding being widely contested, the Druid Order claims a continuous existence from ancient times; the first autumn equinox ritual at Primrose Hill occurred in 1792.

Clypping Ceremony
Painswick, Gloucestershire
23 September

On the Sunday nearest to 19 September the congregation of Painswick gathers for a Clypping ('clasping') ceremony to encircle the church of St Mary the Virgin. The people hold hands and move backwards and forwards, singing the Clypping hymn, surrounded by the ninety-nine splendid yews in the churchyard. A service follows, and every child receives a small cake called a Painswick bun. The ceremony is thought to be a remnant of the Sunday Feast, held on the same date, when Puppy-dog Pie – so-called because the pastry was supported by a china dog – was baked. In the eighteenth century the lord of the manor, Benjamin Hyett, organized an annual procession dedicated to the Lycaean god Pan (the Roman Lupercus); it died out in 1830, but the Classics enthusiast Revd

W.H. Seddon revived festivities in 1897. He believed that a Lupercalia festival (from the Latin for 'wolf') dedicated to Pan was held by Cotswold sheep-farmers, who sacrificed young dogs and goats to intercede for the protection of their flocks from wolves. The Clypping ceremony is thought to be unchanged from this time, and has occurred annually except during the wars. The custom remains as part of the church's patronal service to celebrate the feast day of the Virgin Mary on 8 September. The discrepancy in the dates can be explained by the fact that when the Gregorian calendar was restored in England in 1752 (resulting in a loss of eleven days, 3–13 September), the villagers of Painswick refused to miss their festival; it has been tied to 19 September ever since.

The Original Pearly Kings and Queens Association Harvest Festival

London
7 October

The tradition of pearly kings and queens evolved from the practices of the elected leaders of London costermongers (street traders selling fruit, vegetables, fish etc.). The coster community supported one another by collecting money for those who fell on hard times. 'Pearlies' continue the tradition of helping others by attending various charitable events, including the annual harvest festival at St Martin-in-the-Fields in Trafalgar Square, the proceeds of which are donated to the homeless. The distinctive pearly costume is attributed to Henry Croft, a rat-catcher and road-sweeper, who found a hoard of pearl buttons on the banks of the River Thames in 1875 and used them to decorate a worn-out dress suit. He incorporated patterns and slogans, including 'All for charity' and 'Pity the poor'. As an orphan brought up in the workhouse, he believed in the costers' philanthropic attitude.

Parade of the Ploughmen
Guildford, Surrey
15 October

The World and British National Ploughing Championships are organized by the Society of Ploughmen at a different venue every year, and are contested by 250 ploughing champions from local societies. The aim is to promote the art, skill and science of ploughing the land. There are classes for converted, reversible and horse-drawn ploughs, vintage tractors and horticultural machinery. As well as the contests, there are trade demonstrations, a fairground and rural arts-and-crafts stalls. When the championships have finished, the competing ploughmen take part in a parade, displaying ploughs, tractors and other machinery from various eras.

Apple Day
London
21 October

Apple Day was initiated in 1990 by the environmental charity Common Ground, and has continued every year since, with local communities organizing hundreds of events. Common Ground describes the day as a way of celebrating and demonstrating the importance of local distinctiveness. The charity's aim is to establish an annual custom that links nature with culture and draws attention to the many English apple varieties and related products available throughout the country. Borough Market, on the south bank of the River Thames, marks Apple Day by making available a wide variety of produce and entertaining the crowds with music, theatre and song.

Howgate Wonder

CULINARY, NOVEMBER TO MARCH

BLENHEIM ORANGE X NEWTON WONDER. RAISED IN
1915 – 1916 BY G WRATTON AT HOWGATE LANE,
BEMBRIDGE, ISLE OF WIGHT. IT WAS INTRODUCED
IN 1932 BY STUART LOW CO. RECEIVED AN AWARD
OF MERIT FROM THE RHS IN 1929. FRUITS HAVE
FIRM, FINE/TEXTURED, JUICY FLESH WHICH IS QUITE
SWEET WHEN RIPE WITH A FAINT AROMATIC
FLAVOUR. COOKS WELL.

Punkie Night
Hinton St George, Somerset
27 October

On the last Thursday in October, a 'punkie monarchy' is elected to travel through Hinton St George in a horse-drawn carriage. Children follow it carrying 'punkies', lanterns made from pumpkins and mangel-wurzels with carved faces, stopping at key locations to sing the Punkie Song:

It's Punkie Night tonight!
It's Punkie Night tonight!
Adam and Eve would not believe
It's Punkie Night tonight!

There are obvious references to Hallowe'en trick-or-treat customs in the lines that follow, which include: 'Give me a candle, give me a light. If you don't I'll give you a fright', or 'Give me a candle, give me a light. If you haven't got a candle, a penny's all right.' The festival's origin has been explained by stories of women making lanterns so that they could go after the men of the village who had not returned from Chiselburgh Fair, and by the placing of lanterns on farm gates at this time of year to frighten off evil spirits. After the procession, the punkies are judged in the village hall, and there are also prizes for the best fancy dress.

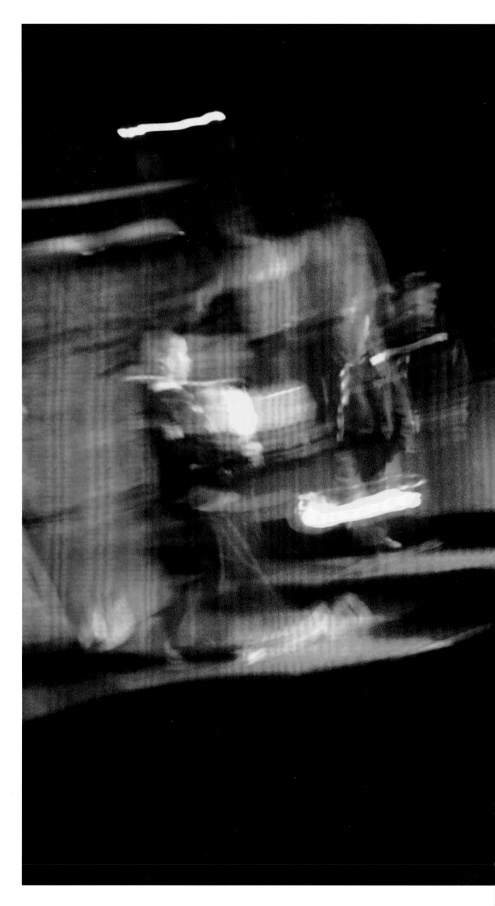

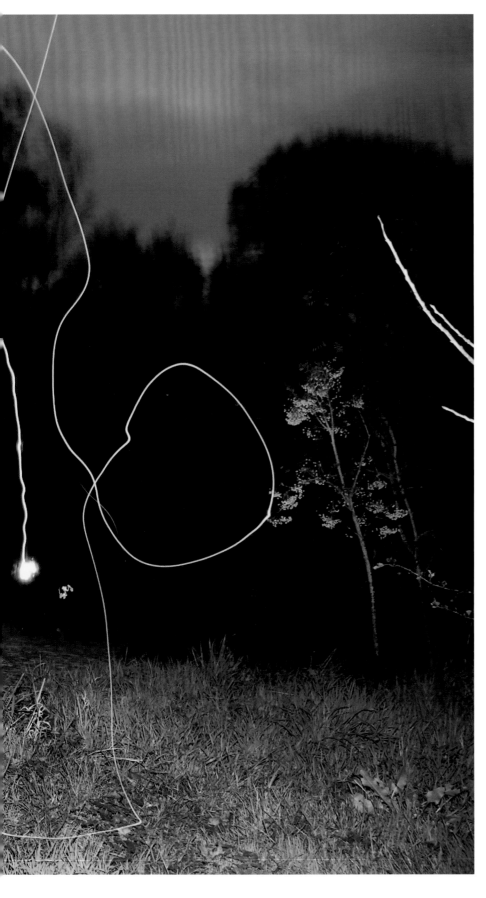

Samhain
Glastonbury, Somerset
31 October

At Samhain, which lasts from sunset on 31 October until midnight on 1 November, a feast was held in pastoral communities all over the country to mark the end of summer. All work on the land was finished, and in that respect the year was complete. Activities varied by region, but Samhain was commonly thought to be a time when supernatural forces were stronger than normal. It is recognized by neo-Pagans as a time to welcome spirits, since the veils of separation between this world and the next are believed to be at their thinnest at this time. Hallowe'en, observed on 31 October, has its roots in Samhain and, subsequently, the Christian festival of All Saints' Day (All Hallows), when prayers are offered for the souls of the dead. At the Chalice Well in Glastonbury, people gather for a programme of events that includes a children's fancy-dress parade, storytelling, music, chanting and a ceremony of giving to the fire and honouring the ancestors.

Antrobus Soulcakers' Play
Antrobus, Cheshire
31 October

Mummers' plays are performed by Morris sides or groups of mummers (see p. 15), which are locally given various names, including 'soulers', 'guisers', 'pace-eggers' and 'plough-stots'. At Hallowe'en the Antrobus Soulcakers, a troupe revived by a former army officer, perform a 'souling' play from pub to pub. Originally, the play (which is particular to Cheshire) was performed by agricultural labourers in return for largesse (usually money) or soul cakes, a rough type of baked parkin traditionally made with oatmeal, molasses and sometimes ginger. 'Soulcaking', as the practice is known, has vestiges of All Hallows' traditions prevalent before the Reformation, and also shares elements with contemporary trick-or-treat customs. The play has a typical hero-combat plot, with the added humour of a Wild Horse character, played by a man covered in sackcloth who operates a wooden horse's head with snapping jaws.

Flaming Tar Barrels
Ottery St Mary, Devon
31 October

There is a long history in the West
Country of carrying flaming tar barrels
through the streets. Possible explanations
include fumigation during the plague, a
warning signal indicating the approach
of the Spanish Armada, or a pagan ritual
to purge evil spirits. The modern event
in Ottery St Mary begins with an early-
morning gun salute and the building of a
huge bonfire, complete with an effigy of
Guy Fawkes. Later, when the light begins
to fade, the first tar-soaked barrels are
ignited and hoisted on to the backs of
'barrel rollers', who run through the
streets. Children carry small barrels; those
carried by adults weigh up to 30 kilograms
(66 lb). Generations of the same family
proudly participate, sponsored by publicans
and individuals who purchase the barrels.
The event is attended by thousands of
spectators, and there are many casualties.
At midnight the barrel-carriers gather to
sing 'Auld Lang Syne', perhaps a reminder
that 1 November was the beginning of
the Celtic New Year.

Bonfire Societies
Sussex
5 November

The forty-one Sussex bonfire societies maintain the ancient tradition of lighting up the dark midwinter nights with fires. Communities participate in costumed torch-lit parades from September to November. Each society has designated costumes, ranging from those of the Wild West to local smugglers' garb. Barcombe in East Sussex has adopted a Japanese theme, while members of one of the five Lewes bonfire societies, Commercial Square Society, have been dressing as Native Americans for 100 years. The society states that this costume was chosen to show solidarity with and protest against the poor treatment of Native Americans, witnessed first-hand by Commercial Square members working on the new railroads. Societies participate in neighbouring parades, adding diversity to the outfits. In Lewes, flaming tar barrels are dragged through the streets on sledges as part of the bonfire celebrations, and are later thrown blazing into the River Ouse. The Lewes celebrations are well known for the controversial practice of burning effigies of 'unpopular' characters, including politicians and the Pope, known as 'Enemies of the Bonfire'. There is also a procession of seventeen burning crosses to commemorate the Sussex Protestant Martyrs who were burned at the stake in the town during the Marian persecutions of 1555–58. Most bonfire societies stage firework displays, and many also hold services of remembrance for lives lost in armed conflict.

Members of bonfire societies drag sledges carrying flaming tar barrels through the streets of Lewes, East Sussex.

Bonfire Societies, Sussex

Lewes Bonfire parade, East Sussex.

Members of the Cliffe Bonfire Society burn an effigy of the Pope, Lewes, East Sussex, 2010.

A burning effigy of David Cameron with Nick Clegg as his puppet, Cliffe Bonfire Society, Lewes, East Sussex, 2010.

Barcombe Bonfire Society parade, East Sussex.

Weston-super-Mare Carnival
Weston-super-Mare, Somerset
15 November

Weston-super-Mare is the last port of call for the Somerset carnivals, which occur throughout the county between August and November. The organizers of the event claim that the earliest newspaper records of it date from 1871, and describe locals with blackened faces banging tin pots and pans. The 'tin-pot bands' would lead a parade to the beach, where effigies of unpopular characters would be burned on bonfires. The tradition of lighting up the dark winter nights continues, but instead of bonfires and live music the people of the town parade to piped music on 130 floats, 50 of which are illuminated with light bulbs. The carnival now boasts 100,000 visitors, and is patrolled by numerous officers from the Health and Safety Executive. It is reported to be the largest illuminated carnival in the world.

St Nicholas-at-Wade Hoodeners
Sandwich, Kent
20 December

Hoodening is primarily thought to be
a tradition from eastern Kent, although
according to Ben Jones, a member of the
St Nicholas-at-Wade Hoodeners, similar
customs exist in Lancashire, Wales, Canada
and Japan. Research by the historian
Ronald Hutton has shown that the
current form dates back to at least 1807,
when agricultural workers would act out
humorous plays at the houses of local
landowners in exchange for money. The
hooden horse, a carved wooden horse's
head mounted on a pole with sackcloth
covering the bearer, played the central
character in performances about death
and rebirth, and is thought by some to
represent the transition from winter to
spring. It is led by a man with a whip or
stick, and is accompanied by a rider, who
frequently tries to mount the horse,
and a Molly, a man dressed as a woman.
The discovery in 1965 of a hooden
horse known as Dobbin in a local attic
instigated the group's revival of hoodening.
During the week before Christmas they
perform a contemporary version of the
traditional folk play, written by the wife
of one of the performers. In 1952 similar
revivals of hoodening were started in
Canterbury, and it is currently practised
in the Whitstable area under the auspices
of the Ancient Order of Hoodeners.

Winter Solstice

Stonehenge, Wiltshire
Primrose Hill, London
Beccles, Suffolk
21 December

Midwinter in the Druid tradition is called Alban Arthan or Alban Arthuan. The name, which is thought to be Brythonic (Celtic) for 'the light of the bear', may refer to the constellation of the Great Bear, which is visible in winter, or to the 'light of Arthur', the mythical king of the British Isles. At the winter solstice people celebrate the imminent return of light as the sun starts to grow in strength. The turn from dark to light is believed by some Druids to be the time of year when the Queen of Heaven, the Great Mother, gave birth to the Son of Light. The midwinter rite often contains the following elements: a call for peace, the forming of a sacred circle, the honouring of the four cardinal points and the ancestors, the placing of offerings, the sharing of bread and mead, and an eisteddfod to which anyone may contribute a poem, song or tale. Lanterns are lit to mark the triumph of summer over winter and of light over darkness.

Above: Offerings placed on the Altar Stone during the Gorsedd of Cor Gawr, Winter Solstice, Stonehenge, Wiltshire.

Right: The Druid Order performs a ritual for the midwinter festival, the Hawthorn Grove, Primrose Hill, London.

Every winter solstice Old Glory dancers and musicians arrive by boat at the Locks Inn public house in Beccles, Suffolk, where they conduct a torch-lit ritual followed by music and dancing. The winter solstice is significant as the day on which the gradual lengthening of nights and shortening of days are reversed, and it is recognized as a time of rebirth. Old Glory formed in 1994 to revive East Suffolk Molly dancing, which is traditionally practised during the winter. The performers are characterized by their blackened faces and heavy farm-labourers' boots, and their robust dance routines are led by a male Lord and Lady. The dancers are all men and the musicians all women.

Herga Mummers
Eastcote, Middlesex
26 December

There are three types of mummers' play, sword, wooing and hero-combat, with regional variations in the costumes, scripts and names of characters. The hero-combat play is the most widespread, with hundreds of versions recorded all over England. Since the 1970s the Herga Mummers, based in Harrow, have performed a revival of the 1850s Middlesex (north-west London) version of the hero-combat play. Typically, the hero, St George, slays a Turkish Knight, who is magically brought back to life by a quack doctor's elixir. Modern scholars say that although the plays incorporate archaic symbols of light and dark and allegories of life, death and rebirth, they probably originated in the early eighteenth century, and are not relics of a pagan fertility ritual (as was once thought by some anthropologists). It is possible, however, that they do preserve echoes of earlier periods. The Herga Mummers jokingly declare that if they didn't perform their ritual drama, 'the crops would fail and the neatly trimmed gardens of London suburbia would become barren'.

The (Insert Name Here) Mummers

Carshalton, Surrey
28 December

Formed in 1999, the (Insert Name Here) Mummers perform traditional mummers' plays around the time of the winter solstice and Christmas festivities. The plays are based on a traditional script, to which the performers add local and contemporary flavour. Members of the troupe are of the opinion that such plays are not of pre-Christian origin, but they do acknowledge the plays' magical symbolism. Mumming is regarded as a valuable form of traditional theatre, bringing live entertainment to pub audiences and beer money to the performers. With humour, the (Insert Name Here) Mummers express this as begging without shame. Their philosophy is: 'We do the play, you enjoy it, you pay us, we don't feel ashamed. Alternatively, we do the play, you don't enjoy it, you pay us to go away and we don't feel ashamed.'

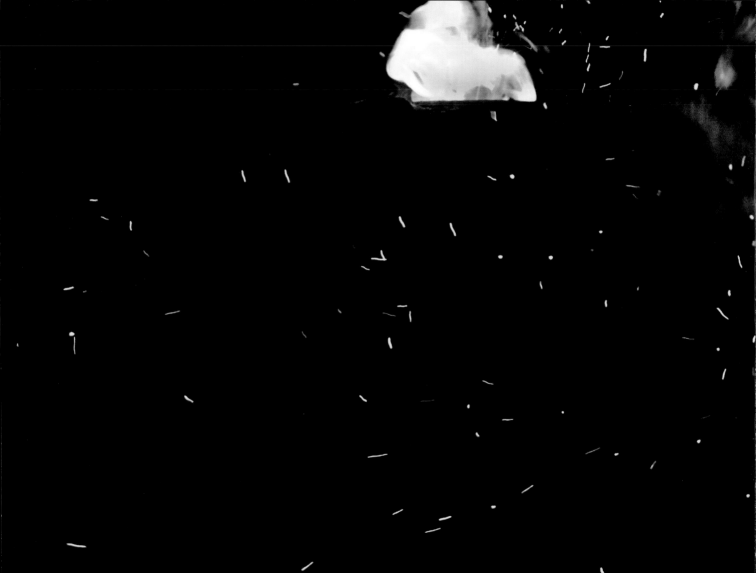

Sources

SELECTED BOOKS

Boyes, G., *The Imagined Village: Culture, Ideology and the English Folk Revival*, Manchester (Manchester University Press) 1993

Bushaway, B., *By Rite: Custom, Ceremony and Community in England 1700–1880*, London (Junction Books) 1982; London (Breviary Stuff Publications) 2011

Cass, E., and Roud, S., *Room, Room, Ladies and Gentlemen: An Introduction to the English Mummers' Play*, London (English Folk Dance and Song Society) 2002

Cawte, E.C., *Ritual Animal Disguise: A Historical and Geographical Study of Animal Disguise in the British Isles*, London (Folklore Society) 1978

Clifford, S., *et al.*, *England in Particular: A Celebration of the Commonplace, the Local, the Vernacular and the Distinctive*, London (Hodder & Stoughton) 2006

Edwards, E., James, P., and Barnes, M., *A Record of England: Sir Benjamin Stone and the National Photographic Record Association, 1897–1910*, Stockport (Dewi Lewis) 2006

Frazer, J., *The Golden Bough: A Study in Magic and Religion*, London (Macmillan) 1890; Ware, Hertfordshire (Wordsworth Editions) 1993

Hobsbawm, E.J., and Ranger, T., *The Invention of Tradition*, Cambridge (Cambridge University Press) 1992

Hutton, R., *The Druids,* London (Hambledon Continuum) 2007

——, *The Pagan Religions of the Ancient British Isles: Their Nature and Legacy*, Oxford (Blackwell) 1991

——, *The Rise and Fall of Merry England: The Ritual Year, 1400–1700*, Oxford (Oxford University Press) 1994

——, *Stations of the Sun: A History of the Ritual Year in Britain*, Oxford (Oxford University Press) 1996

——, *The Triumph of the Moon: A History of Modern Pagan Witchcraft*, Oxford (Oxford University Press) 1999

Judge, R., *The Jack-in-the-Green*, Ipswich, Suffolk (D.S. Brewer) 1979; rev. edn London (FLS Books) 2000

Roberts, R., *Tony Ray-Jones*, London (Chris Boot) 2004

Roud, S., *The English Year: A Month-by-Month Guide to the Nation's Customs and Festivals, from May Day to Mischief Night*, London (Penguin) 2006

Rowe, D., *May Day: The Coming of Spring*, Swindon, Wiltshire (English Heritage) 2006

Straffon, C., *Fentynyow Kernow: In Search of Cornwall's Holy Wells*, Penzance (Meyn Mamvro) 1998

Trubshaw, B., *Explore Folklore*, Loughborough, Leicestershire (Heart of Albion Press) 2002

LIBRARIES AND ARCHIVES

The Folklore Society
The Warburg Institute
Woburn Square
London WC1H 0AB

National Centre for English Cultural Tradition
University of Sheffield
Sheffield S10 2TN

Tony Ray-Jones Archive
National Media Museum
Bradford
West Yorkshire BD1 1NQ

Sir Benjamin Stone Collection
Birmingham Central Library
Chamberlain Square
Birmingham B3 3HQ

Vaughan Williams Memorial Library
English Folk Dance and Song Society
Cecil Sharp House
2 Regent's Park Road
London NW1 7AY

Index

Acknowledgements

In memory of my father

My sincere thanks go to all the people who allowed me to photograph and share in their seasonal rites and customs. I am indebted to Professor Ronald Hutton for his extensive work on the history and current meaning of seasonal rites and rituals; his books are a source of constant inspiration. I should also like to thank Paul Tonkin for helping me to edit my photographs, and June Hannant for her ongoing support. Thank you to Merrell Publishers, especially Hugh Merrell, Nicola Bailey, Dennis Bailey, Alenka Oblak, Rosanna Lewis and Claire Chandler. My gratitude also goes to the Horniman Museum for its enthusiasm for my work, and to the many groups and individuals who have inspired, encouraged and assisted me in the completion of this book, including: Allendale Guisers, Katy Andrews, Geoffrey Appleton, Michael Asbury, Dan Atrill, Sonya Bailey-Gaze, Richard Baker, Anna Basham, Eleanor Bentall, Stefanie Braun, Andrea and Malcolm Broomfield, Tom Brown, Gerard Choy, Shirley Collins, Norma Constable, Carol Cooper, Sarah Crofts, Bill Deld, Ann Dolamore, Dom, James Faure Walker, Fowlers Troop and Deptford Jack-in-the-Green, Kathy Hall, William Hatchett, Mark Hewitson, Mrs D.G. Holliday, Viv Horne, John Hough, Idris and Terri, Dan Keech, Stuart Keegan, Jack Kellett, Andrew Leach, Claire Ludby, Robert McIndoe, Mick McTiernan, Merlin of England, Rodger Molyneux, Jeremy Morgan, Mali Morris, Cheryl Newman, Graham Newson, The 'Nutters', Sarah Oldfield, Jill Pidd, Annie Power, Doc Rowe, John Ryan, Bob Shergold, Jo Summerfield, Peter Symes, Malcolm Taylor, Eckhard Thiemann, Carol Tulloch, Suzana Vaz, Marjorie and Peter Webb, Dave Wells, Mike Wells, Rhonda Wilson, Malcolm Woods and Tony Zandvliet.

A special thank you to Michael Chislett for his passing comment 'There's something good going on at the Dog and Bell tomorrow', without which I would not have encountered Deptford Jack-in-the-Green.

First published 2011 by

Merrell Publishers Limited
81 Southwark Street
London SE1 0HX

merrellpublishers.com

Text and photographs copyright © 2011 Sara Hannant
Design and layout copyright © 2011 Merrell Publishers Limited

British Library Cataloguing-in-Publication data:
Hannant, Sara.
Mummers, maypoles and milkmaids : a journey through the English ritual year.
1. Folk festivals–England–Pictorial works. 2. Rites and ceremonies–England–Pictorial works. 3. England–Social life and customs–Pictorial works.
I. Title
394.2'6942-dc22

ISBN 978-1-8589-4559-0

Produced by Merrell Publishers Limited
Designed by Dennis Bailey
Project-managed by Rosanna Lewis
Indexed by Hilary Bird
Printed and bound in China

Jacket, front: The Holly Man, Twelfth Night Celebrations, Bankside, London (pp. 18–19)
Jacket, back, clockwise from top left: Horn Dance, Abbots Bromley, Staffordshire (pp. 108–11); Jack-in-the-Green, Hastings, East Sussex (pp. 44–49); Flaming Tar Barrels, Ottery St Mary, Devon (pp. 132–33); Whitsuntide, Bampton, Oxfordshire (pp. 70–71)
Frontispiece: The Fool, Abbots Bromley Horn Dance (pp. 108–11)
Pages 6–7: The Red Leicester Morrismen at the Whittlesey Straw Bear Festival, Cambridgeshire (pp. 20–23)
Pages 154–55: 'Barrel roller', Ottery St Mary, Devon (pp. 132–33)
Page 160: A member of Abingdon Traditional Morris Dancers (pp. 78–81)